The ingredients of glass are very simple; **SAND** (known as silica) **SODA** (known as Sodium Carbonate) and **LIME** (known as lime). These ingredients, when heated properly, turn into glass. The addition of various metal oxides gives us colored glass.

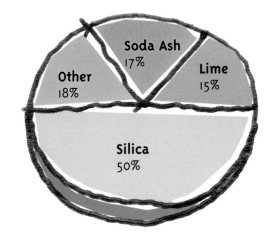

Materials Used in the Manufacturing of Glass

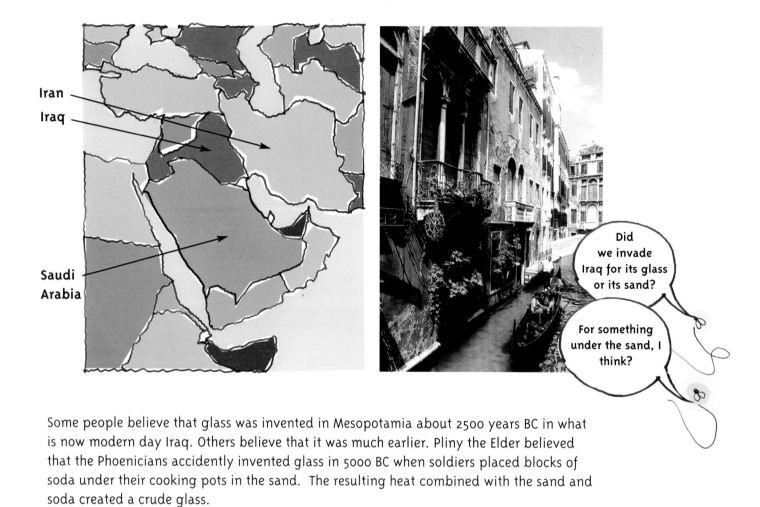

Iran

Iraq

Saudi
Arabia

Did we invade Iraq for its glass or its sand?

For something under the sand, I think?

Some people believe that glass was invented in Mesopotamia about 2500 years BC in what is now modern day Iraq. Others believe that it was much earlier. Pliny the Elder believed that the Phoenicians accidently invented glass in 5000 BC when soldiers placed blocks of soda under their cooking pots in the sand. The resulting heat combined with the sand and soda created a crude glass.

By 1000 AD glass was more common and much of it was produced in Venice. But it wasn't until 1600 that the French began using it for windows and mirrors. Glazing was born!!!

Over the next few hundred years glazing technologies didn't change much other than a gradual improvement in the quality of the glass and frames. **DOUBLE AND TRIPLE GLAZING** was patented in 1865 by Thomas Stetson, but that technology wasn't common until the 1960's and 1970's.

So until recently, there really was only one type of glazing that you could have selected Sidney.

That must be what I was thinking of!

That's right Jeffrey, until very recently architects like Sidney used the same general type of glazing on every type of building regardless of what it was and where it was. Windows were always of the **SINGLE PANE VARIETY** and you can still find them everywhere on older buildings.

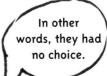

In other words, they had no choice.

Sidney has a lot of choices!

Since it was difficult to make quality glass that was very big, windows were usually comprised of several small panes of glass called **LITES**, creating the familiar look of older windows.

Yah...these windows were called true divided lites since the frame separated each piece of glass.

Why is it called a lite?

Lite

Why are you called a fly? Stop asking stupid questions!

While this type of glazing looked good, it was not the best solution for our windows. The energy performance of the windows were poor, so it took more energy to keep the building comfortable. The more energy a building uses, the more environmental impact is created and the more money is spent.

Nowadays it is possible to get a wide variety of glass for just about any need. We are no longer limited to just a few options. So what are the options? Turn the page to find out!

When selecting glazing there are four major properties that you look for.

The four properties are:

- **U-VALUE**

- **SOLAR HEAT GAIN COEFFICIENT (SHGC)**

- **VISIBLE LIGHT TRANSMITTANCE (VLT)**

- **AIR LEAKAGE RATE**

U-VALUE is the measure of the rate of non-solar heat loss and gain through the material, otherwise known as **CONDUCTION**. U-value is the inverse of an **R-VALUE**, which measures the resistance (R) of a material to heat flow. For example an R-value of 2 is the same as a u-value of 0.5. The higher the R-value the better the material is as an insulator. The lower the u-value the better an insulator as well. Glazing is measured with u-value while most 'solid' materials are reported as R-values. A u-value is typically expressed in **BTU/HR-SF** (British Thermal Units/hour/sf) in this country. For most glazing today u-values typically fall between 0.2-1.2 (R 0.8 - R-5)

Window Description	Center-of-Glass U-factor (BTU/hr-ft2-F)	Overall U-factor (BTU/hr-ft2-F)
1 Single Glass Aluminum Frame with no thermal break	1.11	1.30
5 Double Glass Wood / Vinyl frame	0.49	0.49
9 Double Glass Select low-E (.04)-argon Wood / Vinyl frame	0.24	0.29
11 Triple glass Low-E (2 surfaces)-krypton Insulated Vinyl frame	0.11	0.15

This drawing illustrates heat loss by conduction through the window in winter combined with radiation and air movement (convection) on the surfaces of the glazing. The u-factor of a window is a combination of these conductive, convective, and radiative heat transfer mechanisms.

All this math is making my head hurt!

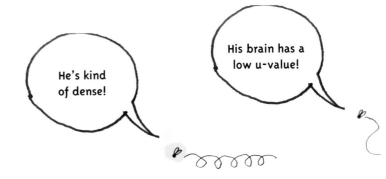

He's kind of dense!

His brain has a low u-value!

The next property to examine is the **VISIBLE LIGHT TRANSMITTANCE (VLT).**

Visible light transmittance is the fraction of the visible electromagnetic spectrum that is transmitted through the glazing. It is expressed as a PERCENTAGE!

That's right Jeffrey. Visual light transmittance is a measure of how much light will make it through the glass. A clear single pane window has a vlt close to 90%. Modern glass has a lower light transmittance because there is more 'material' for light to travel through, usually two panes of glass with coatings and sometimes gas fills. Most glazing units range between 40%-70% VLT.

You're right Jeffrey. Forgive me. Again, visual light transmittance is a measure of how much incident light makes it through the pane of glass. Some light is **REFLECTED**, some light is **INTERNALLY REFRACTED** and the rest makes it through. Clear modern glass might have a vlt of 0.75 which means that 75% of the light makes it through. A heavily tinted glass might have a vlt of 0.45, which means only 45% of the light makes it through.

The third property to examine is the **SOLAR HEAT GAIN COEFFICIENT (SHGC)**.

SHGC is a measure of how much heat makes it through the glass to the interior of the building compared to the amount that strikes it. You can select glass to control the amount of heat that the windows permit.

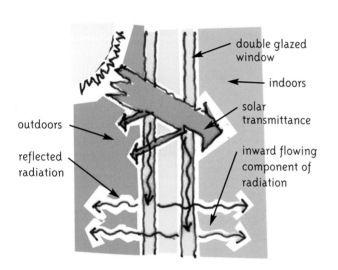

double glazed window

indoors

solar transmittance

inward flowing component of radiation

outdoors

reflected radiation

What do you mean heat? I thought we were talking about light?

Light always comes with heat Sidney...you should know that!

This is getting pretty technical!

And groovy! I can see that ultraviolet stuff!

Right again Jeffrey. Light from the sun has three components; **ULTRAVIOLET LIGHT (RADIATION)**, **VISIBLE LIGHT** and **INFRARED RADIATION**.

RADIATION is the transfer of heat in the form of electromagnetic waves from one surface to another. The Solar Heat Gain Coefficient (SHGC) is a number that describes how much solar radiation is admitted through a window directly or that which is absorbed and then re-radiated inwards. It is expressed as a value between 0 and 1. The lower the number, the less heat is transmitted.

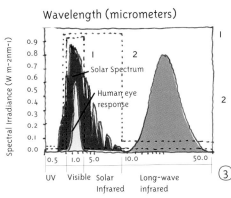

Wavelength (micrometers)

1 Idealized transmittance of a spectrally selective glazing designed for low solar heat gain. Visible light is transmitted and near infrared solar radiation is reflected (suitable for a warm climate).

2 Idealized transmittance of a low-e glazing designed for high solar heat gain. Visible light and near infrared solar radiation is transmitted. Far-infrared radiation is reflected back into the interior (suitable for a cold climate).

③

There is much more to light than meets the eye!

Especially if you are a fly!!!

Effect of solar heat gain coefficient (SHGC) on annual cooling season energy performance.

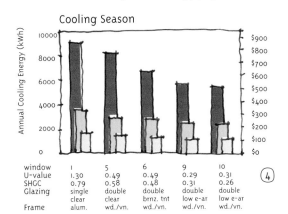

Cooling Season

☐ Madison, WI (3343 CDH)
☐ St. Louis, MO (17,843 CDH)
■ Phoenix, AZ (54,404 CDH)

④

window	1	5	6	9	10
U-value	1.30	0.49	0.49	0.29	0.31
SHGC	0.79	0.58	0.48	0.31	0.26
Glazing	single clear	double clear	double brnz. tnt	double low e-ar	double low e-ar
Frame	alum.	wd./vn.	wd./vn.	wd./vn.	wd./vn.

Another number that is often discussed is that of a window's **SHADING COEFFICIENT (SC)** which measures a window's ability to block solar heat relative to clear glass. It is equal to the SHGC x 1.15. Basically the sc number has been replaced by the glazing industry by the SHGC.

The final property that we need to learn is the **AIR LEAKAGE RATE (ALR)**. The ALR is a measure of how much leakage (**INFILTRATION**) exists around a window, door, or skylight with a known specific pressure difference. It is shown in units of cubic feet/ minute/ square foot of frame area. The lower the number, the tighter, or less 'leaky' the window.

Infiltration through cracks in the window assembly is another mechanism for energy transfer.

National Fenestration
Rating Council ⑤

Right again, Jeffrey. The **NFRC** is a national non-profit, comprised of members in the public and private arenas. The group has members who are manufacturers, suppliers, builders, architects and government agencies. They've come together to help people compare apples to apples with products. Their label demonstrates how each product rates in the four areas that we discussed a second ago. It's very simple. Each window or skylight manufacturer is required to show the performance characteristics of their product in the same way as determined by the NFRC.

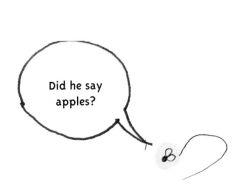

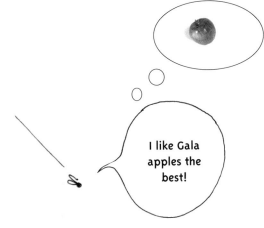

Glazing units get their properties from a variety of methods that we will explain in this section. In general they come from the following five main methods:

- **COATINGS**

- **AIRSPACE THICKNESS**

- **GAS FILLS**

- **NUMBER OF GLASS UNITS OR AIRSPACES**

- **FRAME MATERIAL**

The first issue has to do with the number of glass layers that make up the window.

Going from one layer of glass (a single pane window) to two with a 1/4 inch airspace increases the center of glass R-value from .9 to 1.75.

At least there isn't any French onion soup!!

I still don't see any apples!

The important thing to know is that glass itself has very poor insulating properties. Indeed, it is not the glass itself that provides its insulating properties but the **BOUNDARY LAYER** of air that surrounds the glass.If you disturb this boundary layer too much the glass will temporarily lose more heat! A double pane window is vastly superior to a single pane window, not because of the extra glass, but because of the airspace between them. Increasing the **AIRSPACE** to 1/2" increases the R-value even more.

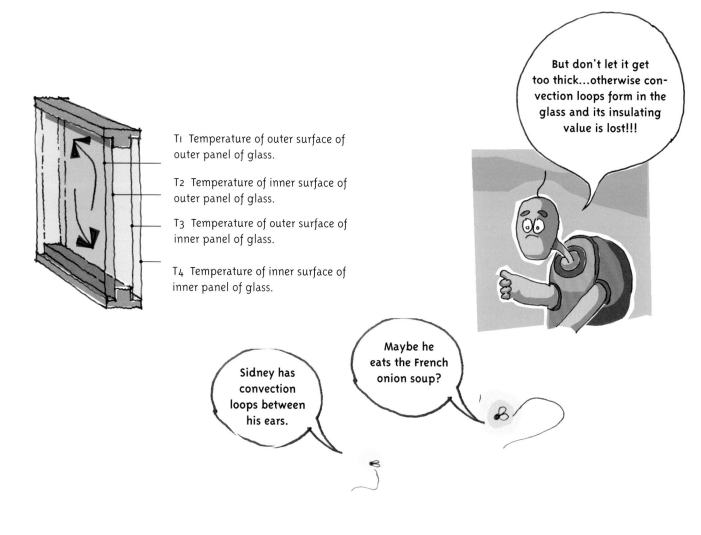

T1 Temperature of outer surface of outer panel of glass.

T2 Temperature of inner surface of outer panel of glass.

T3 Temperature of outer surface of inner panel of glass.

T4 Temperature of inner surface of inner panel of glass.

So if you want to increase a glazing unit's u-value, one way is to add more layers. But it doesn't have to just be glass, as too many layers of glass make the window too thick. Some manufacturers suspend a **TRANSPARENT FILM** between two layers of glass providing an additional air space without creating a really thick window and lowering the u-value even further. Either way, remember that the more layers the light has to travel through, the more the amount of visible light is also affected.

So as u-values are improved, visible light transmittance drops slightly.

Heat Mirror Film

Two air spaces

HEAT MIRROR

The u-value is also affected by the frame that the glass sits in. In fact, it is usually the weak link in the system as heat can flow uninterrupted through the frame. If the frame is metal it conducts a lot of heat and the window's performance really suffers. Wood is a better insulator. Manufacturers now make '**THERMALLY-BROKEN**' frames that impede heat flow. This is an important point because you should always know if the u-value for the window is just for the glass (known as center of glass rating) or total unit. Total unit is what you need to know!

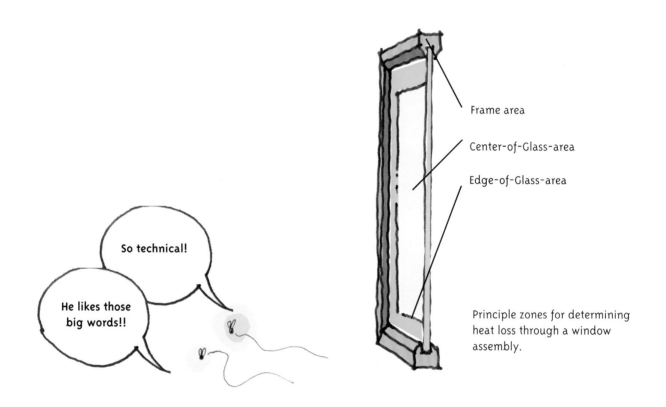

Frame area

Center-of-Glass-area

Edge-of-Glass-area

Principle zones for determining heat loss through a window assembly.

So technical!

He likes those big words!!

Yes, Jeffrey, getting right to that. Another way that a window gets its insulating property is by changing the nature of the airspace between the glass panes using another type of gas.

Windows typically have two types of **GAS FILLS** that improve the thermal performance: **ARGON** and **KRYPTON**. Both are inert, non-toxic gases that can be injected into the airspace. Argon is cheaper, but less effective than krypton in insulating the glazing unit. A double pane window without a gas fill MIGHT have a u-value of 0.48; with the gas the new value MIGHT be 0.33.

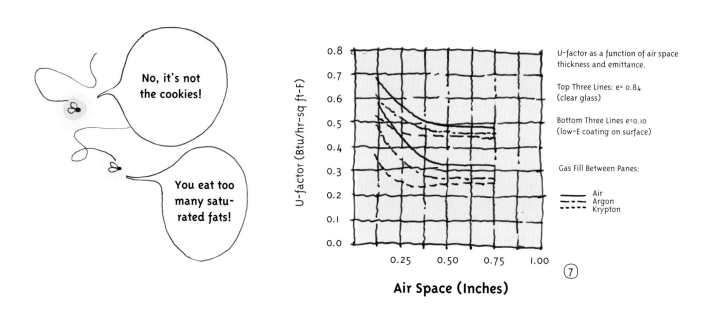

No, it's not the cookies!

You eat too many saturated fats!

U-factor as a function of air space thickness and emittance.

Top Three Lines: e= 0.84 (clear glass)

Bottom Three Lines e=0.10 (low-E coating on surface)

Gas Fill Between Panes:

——— Air
-·-·- Argon
- - - Krypton

Air Space (Inches)

But even more important than the gas fills is the presence of coatings on the glass. Coatings are generally known as **LOW-E COATINGS**, which means **LOW EMISSIVITY**.

Low-e coatings were developed in the 1970's and came to the market in 1980. Emissivity is the ability of a surface to emit radiant energy with the glass absorbing part of the energy by radiating it away from the surface.

Low-e coatings are thin, virtually invisible metal or **METALLIC OXIDE LAYERS** deposited on a glass surface. Typically, they are used to impede heat flow through the glass and improve the u-value of the unit. They also can have a dramatic effect on the SHGC of the window depending on where the coating is located.

First explain how they are applied!

Low emittance coatings can be applied in two different ways; as a **HARD COAT**, called a **PYROLITIC** or a **SOFT COAT**, known as a **SPUTTER COAT**.

Hard coat coatings (pyrolytic) have a thin layer of tin oxide incorporated into the surface of the glass as it's made...hence the fire reference. It is a very durable coating and is typically used on outside surfaces, but it is not nearly as good at insulating as the soft coat and lets heat in more readily. This may be okay for a solar building, but not good if heat gain is a problem.

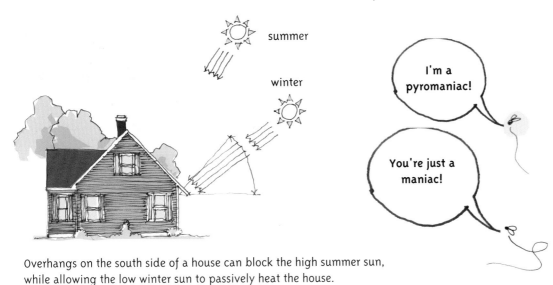

summer

winter

I'm a pyromaniac!

You're just a maniac!

Overhangs on the south side of a house can block the high summer sun, while allowing the low winter sun to passively heat the house.

Soft coats, otherwise known as sputter coats, use thin layers of silver and anti-reflective components that are applied to the surface through a vacuum deposition process. Since the coating is delicate it stays on the inside of a sealed unit. These coatings can also be applied to **SUSPENDED FILMS** as well.

Special versions of these coatings have even been designed to target specific wavelengths of light, usually to let in the visible spectrum (**SHORT WAVE**) but to block the heat gain component (**LONG WAVE**)...this is called **SPECTRALLY SELECTIVE GLASS**.

Spectrally selective glass might have a high vlt and a low SHGC for example. With normal coatings, as the SHGC drops so does the vlt.

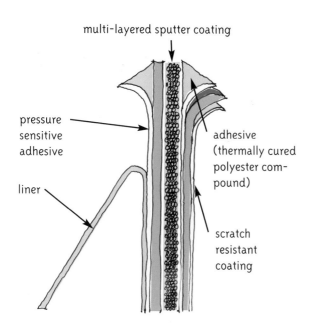

multi-layered sputter coating

pressure
sensitive
adhesive

liner

adhesive
(thermally cured
polyester com-
pound)

scratch
resistant
coating

As briefly mentioned, a wide variety of characteristics can be achieved depending on where certain coatings appear. Surfaces are typically numbered as in the diagram to the right.

If the coating is on the third surface, glass absorbs the heat striking it and it gets warm. Since the low emissivity coating prevents it from re-radiating back out, all the heat goes inward, which is good for solar gain. In other words, it reflects the heat back into the room. If the low-e coating is on the inside of the outer layer on surface two it will block more heat and have an improved SHGC.

Surface Reference Diagram

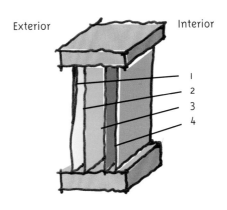

Exterior   Interior
1
2
3
4

Now wait just a minute....with all these coatings how does it affect the way my glass looks? Remember, I care for aesthetics!

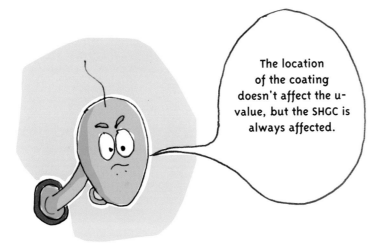

The location of the coating doesn't affect the u-value, but the SHGC is always affected.

That's an important point, Sidney. Coatings do affect the way the glass looks through some type of coloration, although more and more coatings are being developed that are 'clear' and don't change aesthetics a great deal.

But in general, an architect should request samples from the glass manufacturer to see the color implications...especially if different types of glass are used on the same building or facades (as we will recommend later). Even 'clear' glass has some sort of color.

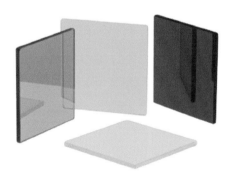

Common colors for 'tints' are grey, green, blue and bronze. Grey glass typically transmits approximately equal visible light and infrared light. Bronze tends to let in less visible and more infrared than grey. Blue and green glass transmit more visible light and less infrared than grey.

And with that, we are finished with our discussion of how glazing gets its properties!

So it's simple. When you select glass you need to know its visual light transmittance, its solar heat gain coefficient, its air leakage rate, and its u-value. But what I want to know is why I wouldn't just pick a combination I like and use it everywhere?

Come on Sidney. Think a little bit here!!!

Well, that is what a lot of architects do Sidney, but you need to be smarter! The window type you select should be based on a variety of factors....

Can you get high from sniffing argon?

Let's try to find out.

There are many factors that can affect the selection
of glazing on a project, some of the important ones
are listed below:

- **BUILDING TYPE**

- **CLIMATE**

- **AESTHETICS**

- **VIEWS & CONNECTION TO OUTDOORS**

- **SITE CONDITIONS**

- **ORIENTATION**

- **SHADING DEVICES & LIGHT SHELVES**

- **AMOUNT OF GLAZING**

- **DAYLIGHTING**

One of the most important factors in selecting glazing is the building type. This topic is so complex that it deserves a handbook itself. The topic is what I call **'BUILDING BEHAVIOR'** or the study of how a building's operating characteristics should inform the design of the building.

To simplify this topic as much as possible, we can break it down into saying that buildings are either internally load dominated or externally load dominated.

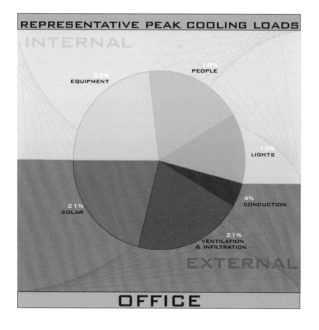

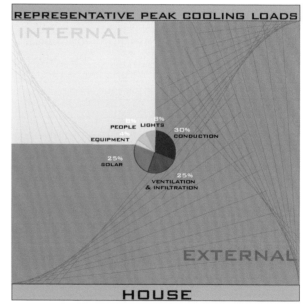

An **INTERNALLY LOAD DOMINATED BUILDING** is a large building that has so many internal loads from lighting, equipment and people that it dominates how the building has to be conditioned. Outside temperatures play a smaller role. This type of building typically needs cooling all year round, even in cool climates.

⑨

An **EXTERNALLY LOAD DOMINATED BUILDING** is a small building with a lot of perimeter surface area. The outside conditions dominate how the building is conditioned. In most climates in the winter it needs lots of heating; in the summer, lots of cooling.

An internally load dominated building needs glass that is good at letting in light to reduce internal lighting loads, but also that is good at blocking heat gain since it always needs cooling...no sense adding more heat to cool!!

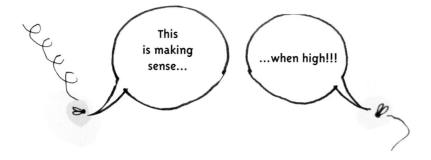

An externally load dominated building likely needs heat in the winter, so you might want to select a glass with a SHGC that permits heat. A really good u-value is also critical.

The next thing to consider is the **CLIMATE**. For example, the harsher the climate the more important it is to have a good u-value and air leakage rate. Otherwise, you spend a lot of money keeping the building comfortable! The right SHGC is also critical.

After that is aesthetics, but since we already discussed how glazing can have different colors and tints we can move on.

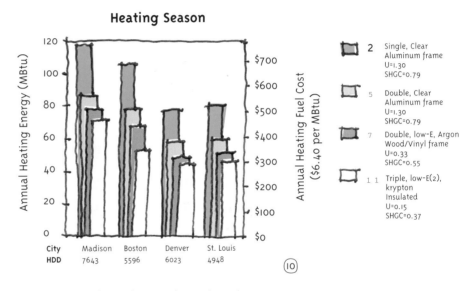

Heating Season

City	Madison	Boston	Denver	St. Louis
HDD	7643	5596	6023	4948

2 Single, Clear Aluminum frame U=1.30 SHGC=0.79

5 Double, Clear Aluminum frame U=1.30 SHGC=0.79

7 Double, low-E, Argon Wood/Vinyl frame U=0.33 SHGC=0.55

1 1 Triple, low-E(2), krypton Insulated U=0.15 SHGC=0.37

(10)

Note: The annual energy performance figures show here are for a typical 1540 sqft. house. U-factor and SHGC are for total window including frame.

The fourth factor is that of **VIEWS AND CONNECTION TO THE OUTSIDE**. The lower the vlt the darker the glass. If the glass gets too dark, it has the potential to diminish the connection to the outside and views from inside the building.

But keep in mind that glass can appear very dark on the outside, but still appear quite bright from inside!

ORIENTATION is another critical factor affecting glazing selection. East and West facing windows can present blinding glare and hard to control **HEAT GAIN**. Glass should be chosen to mitigate these effects through its vlt and SHGC! North facing glass 'sees' less of the direct sun but also has less light for the interior...increasing the vlt might become important in that case.

What we need soon is a cartoon guide to daylighting design.

I'm sure its coming!!!

South facing windows offer a great deal of light, but also potential heat gain problems if not properly addressed...which brings us to the next factor...

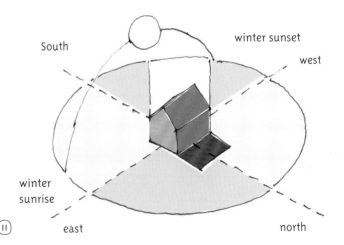

SHADING DEVICES - If sunlight can be properly controlled through the use of overhangs, light shelves and fins then it opens up the possibility for a wider range of options. For example, with good overhangs, a passive solar house could keep out unwanted heat gain in the summer and allow heat to enter in the winter through glass with a high SHGC.

Seems like this could spin off another guide book?

The passive solar book! The topics are endless!

The next factor is that of **SITE CONDITIONS**...for example, the building shown on this page has a large expanse of west facing glass...however, it sits right next to a giant stand of old growth trees that block all west facing direct sun...so instead of needing a low vlt and a low shgc it can enjoy a high vlt with great views of the forest and the SHGC is not really an issue!

Always design based on site conditions Sidney!!!

Design for place!

Bio-regionalism!!!

⑫

The final factor in choosing glazing is related to the overall topic of **DAYLIGHTING**, which is the art and science of using daylight as a light source in a building. Like a few other things mentioned, this is a whole topic unto itself...it takes a lot of skill to use glazing well! But, in general, what is important to know right now is that the type of glazing needs to match the specific requirements of the room behind it. In a working environment like an office, uniform lighting conditions are desirable...choosing the right glass to avoid glare becomes important. If the room in question is a lobby, glare is not as big of an issue; more contrast in lighting conditions might actually be a good thing...it all depends!

All right Sidney, we'll see if we can pull all of this together. Let's take a look at two buildings and you can decide how we might select glazing for it. I will give you a few window options to choose from...kind of like a multiple choice exam!

Remember all the factors you need to consider!!! Especially Climate, Orientation and Building Type.

Glazing Chart

Type	U-Value	VLT	SHGC
A	0.30	73%	.93
B	1.09	89%	.81
C	0.26	78%	.75
D	0.48	21%	.035
E	0.29	70%	.37

* based on products currently available

Let's pick one climate so that you get the picture, say, **KANSAS CITY**. Kansas City has a challenging climate. It can get cold in the wintertime, but it also gets really hot and humid in the summertime. Now let's look at two different building types, a **LARGE OFFICE BUILDING** and a **HOUSE**.

Let's look at the house first and consider the two windows that are highlighted. What do you think we should do?

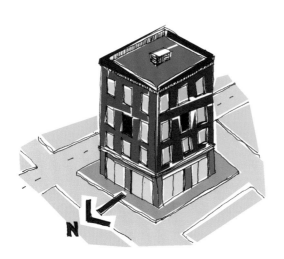

Ok, Mr.Narrator....well, since the house is an externally load dominated building it needs heating in the wintertime and cooling in summertime. The first window is facing south, while the second window is facing west. The house seems to have good overhangs on the south side, and there are a lot of trees in front of the west window.

Wow! He's not so dumb after all!

So it's pretty simple. I would choose glass type A for the south window because it has a good u-value and the SHGC is high to permit solar gain in the winter which is what I want! In fact, I bet that low-e coating is on the third surface.

Since the trees block the west facing sun I'm not really worried about the SHGC. So, I might pick glass type C since it also has a real good u-value and a higher VLT to make up for the blocked light from the trees.

Type	U-Value	VLT	SHGC
A	0.30	73%	.93
B	1.09	89%	.81
C	0.26	78%	.75
D	0.48	21%	.035
E	0.29	70%	37

That's really good Sidney!!!

Now for the office building!

The office building is an internally load dominated building and this one doesn't seem to have any exterior sunshades anywhere!!! Kind of looks like a lot of buildings I've designed. The first window is facing west which could really be a problem for us...the second window is facing north.

For the west facing window I might consider glass D since it has a low vlt, which might help a bit with glare and a really low SHGC to keep out that unwanted heat. But that would also give me a heavy tint, which I'm not sure I want....so, out of these few choices I'd probably select glass type E which looks like a spectrally selective glass. Its VLT is pretty high, while its SHGC is pretty low. That might be a good balance, although too bright at times.

Type	U-Value	VLT	SHGC
A	0.30	73%	.93
B	1.09	89%	.81
C	0.26	78%	.75
D	0.48	21%	.035
E	0.29	70%	37

N

For the north facing window I could select the same spectrally selective glass, or I could go with something that has an even higher VLT to let in more light....so many options!!!

He's using some big words now!

Yaah, and they make sense!

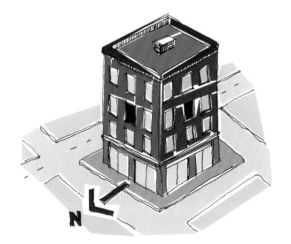

Type	U-Value	VLT	SHGC
A	0.30	73%	.93
B	1.09	89%	.81
C	0.26	78%	.75
D	0.48	21%	.035
E	0.29	70%	37

That's right Sidney, and what we are going through is just the beginning of the thought process. To select glazing properly it is usually wise to look at how different glazing selections will affect **ENERGY PERFORMANCE** through the use of **ENERGY MODELS** that your engineer can provide you with. A good energy model can help you understand how the heating and cooling loads will be affected through the decisions you make. But the process you just went through should get you closer to the right answer each time.

The other tool that can help make this even more scientific is the use of **DAYLIGHTING MODELS** that can either be done on computer or through scale models. These models can help you determine how effective your glazing choices are relative to using daylight as the lightsource. A daylighting consultant can help you with these choices.

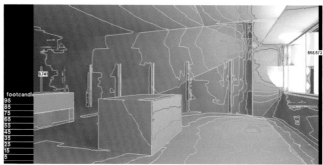

So those are the basics Sidney. All that's left to discuss is the future. Glazing technologies are ever evolving and there are a lot of exciting things in store for the industry. Before we go we can mention a few of them.

The first is **SUPER GLAZING**. With the right combinations of glass, suspended films, coatings and gas fills it's possible to achieve R values between 6 and 10 (u-0.16 - 0.10) which can make a huge difference in the energy performance of externally load dominated buildings. Super glazing is not really new, but because of the first cost premium it is not yet in widespread use. The time has come for more projects to select this type of window product!

The second is **SMART GLASS**. There are different types of 'smart-glass' available in limited amounts today. What they share is the ability of the glass to change its properties depending on either the outside temperature conditions or desired inside conditions.

That sounds great!

ELECTROCHROMIC GLASS is the most promising of these technologies. Electrochromic glass is able to change from a totally clear state to a totally opaque state with nearly infinite degrees of opacity in between. Users would be able to operate the window like a dimmer on a light depending on whether they want light and heat to enter the room or not. An electric current runs through the glazing to create the change in state. The electrochromic glass could also be tied to the building's mechanical system to help the building regulate comfort!

High-Transmission State (clear)

Electrolyte

Passive counter electrode

Solar Energy transmitted

Active ElectroChromic Layer

Transparent Conductor

Lithium Ions

Voltage Source

Low-Transmission State (Colored)

Passive counter electrode

Solar Energy partially transmitted

Solar Energy Rejected

Active ElectroChromic Layer

Transparent conductor

Reverse Voltage

Schematic diagram of a five layer electrochromic coating (not to scale). A reversible low-voltage source moves ions back and forth between an active electrochromic layer and a passive counterelectrode.

Fantastic!!!!

Superb!!!!

The future also holds the potential for **THERMOCHROMICS**...glazing that responds to temperature fluctuations and modulates its properties...in other words, a window might be clear during overcast skies, but when the sun comes out it heats the surface of the glass and the glass might change properties in order to block heat.

The final technology that we will mention is that of transparent **PHOTOVOLTAICS**. Photovoltaics are the same as 'solar panels' and are a solid state technology capable of generating electricity from sunlight. Test installations have been done for transparent photovoltaics that will allow some amount of light to travel through the solar panels while also generating electricity. Imagine that!!!!

For more information and where to go next, see the resources section of the book. Until Next Time!!!

FINI

Franta, Gregory, Kristin Arstead & Greg D. Ander. *The AIA Glazing Design Handbook for efficiency*, Southern California Edison, 1997

Efficient Windows Collaborative, www.efficient windows.org

Energy Users News - Glazing for Savings dec. 08/2000 - Greg Franta, FAIA, www.energyuses.com

Environmental Building News, March/April 1996 Volume 5 Number 2
Windows: Looking Through the Options

How Buildings Behave, Jason F. McLennan, (Online Publication) Environmental Design and Construction 2002

National Fenestration Ratings Council Website, www.nfrc.org

Viracon Website, www.viracon.com

AIR LEAKAGE RATE — A measure of how much air leakage exists around a window, door or skylight with a known specific pressure difference. Expressed in cubic feet/minute/square foot of frame area. The lower the number the 'tighter the construction'.

ARGON — An inert colorless gas that is inserted between glass to improve the thermal performance of a window assembly.

BUILDING BEHAVIOR — The science of predicting energy usage and heating and cooling loads based on a building's climate and type. Coined by the Author.

BLT SANDWICH — A particularly tasty sandwich that consists of lettuce, tomato and bacon between bread. Mayo is usually added for additional flavor. Turkey Bacon may be substituted for normal bacon for a greatly reduced fat content.

BOUNDARY LAYER — A thin layer of still air that clings to a surface. In glazing, the boundary layer improves the thermal resistance of the window assembly.

BRITISH THERMAL UNITS (BTU) — A measure of heat in the Imperial system. A BTU is the power required to produce energy at the rate of 1 joule per second. 1 watt = 3.412 BTU/h Conduction — Heat flow through a material. Measured in BTU/h/sf

CONVECTION — Heat flow through air.

DOUBLE GLAZING — A window assembly with two panes of glass.

DUMB ARCHITECT — An oxymoron, since Architects are never dumb! However, a powerful reminder that architects do a lot of dumb things!

EXTERNALLY LOAD DOMINATED BUILDING — A small building with a high surface to volume ratio. These building types have heating and cooling loads driven primarily by external factors.

ELECTROCHROMIC GLASS — Smart Glazing that has been engineered to respond to an electric current to change its opacity and translucency.

FRENCH ONION SOUP — A wonderfully tasty consume soup filled with caramelized onions and a heavy dose of Gruyere cheese. Deadly to flies.

INFRARED LIGHT — Light that contains shorter wavelengths of light than light in the visible spectrum and is thus invisible to the human eye.

INTERNALLY LOAD DOMINATED BUILDING — A Large building with a low surface to volume ratio. These building types have heating and cooling loads driven by internal factors such as lights and equipment.

INTERNAL REFRACTION — Light that is bounced and lost within glass. Usually dwarfed by the percentage of light that is reflected or transmitted through.

KRYPTON — A destroyed planet that once was home to a race of superhuman beings. Also, an inert colorless gas that is inserted between glass to improve the thermal performance of a window assembly. It is unknown if these two definitions are somehow related.

LOW E- COATINGS — An invisible coating applied to glass to improve its thermal characteristics. E stands for emmissivity, which is the ability of a material to emit radiant energy.

PHOTOVOLTAICS — A solid-state technology that converts sunlight into electricity.

PYROLITIC COATINGS (HARD COATS) — A coating applied to glass while being manufactured that improves its thermal properties.

R-VALUE — Stands for Resistance Value and is a measure of a material's ability to resist heat flow.

SHADING COEFFICIENT (SC) — A measure that describes a window's ability to block heat relative to clear glass.

SINGLE GLAZING — A window assembly with only a single pane of glass. Usually very lonely.

SOLAR HEAT GAIN CO-EFFICIENT (SHGC) — A measure that describes how much heat makes it through the glass compared to the amount that strikes it.

SPECTRALLY SELECTIVE GLAZING — Glazing that selectively blocks certain wavelengths of light more readily than others. Typically designed to block heat while permitting visible light.

SPUTTER COATINGS (SOFT COATS) — A coating placed on windows after they have been cooled to improve the thermal performance of the glass.

SUPER GLAZING — Windows with R-values over 6.

SUSPENDED FILMS — A thin transparent 'plastic-like' sheet that is suspended between two or more panes of glass to create additional air spaces without introducing thickness to the assembly.

THERMALLY BROKEN FRAMES — A window frame that utilizes a change of material from the inside to the outside in order to impede heat flow by conduction through the material. Thermally broken frames are particularly important with metal window frames.

THERMOCHROMIC GLASS — Glass that has been chemically designed to change opacity and translucency in response to the surface temperature of the glass.

TRIPLE GLAZING — A window assembly with three panes of glass.

U-VALUE — A measure of the rate of heat loss and gain through a material by conduction typically expressed in BTU/hr-sf.

ULTRAVIOLET LIGHT — Light outside the visible light spectrum.

VISIBLE LIGHT TRANSMITTANCE (VLT) — A measure of the amount of light that makes it through glass as compared to the amount striking the surface. Expressed as a percentage.

VLT SANDWICH — A bad pun combining 'visible light transmittance and BLT sandwich. See BLT sandwich.

Cover Image ©2002 Assassi Productions. Photo
courtesy of BNIM Architects.

1 Copyright © Mike Sinclair. Photo courtesy of
   BNIM Architects.

2 Copyright © Mike Sinclair. Photo courtesy of
   BNIM Architects.

3 Adapted from AIA Glazing Design Handbook

4 Adapted from AIA Glazing Design Handbook

5 National Fenestration Ratings Council

6 Southwall

7 Adapted from AIA Glazing Design Handbook

8 Copyright © BNIM Architects

9 Copyright © Mike Sinclair.Photo courtesty of
   BNIM Architects.

10 Adapted from AIA Glazing Design Handbook

11 Photo courtesy of Keen Engineering

12 Copyright © Mike Sherman. Photo courtesy
   Matsusaki Wright

13 Copyright © BNIM Architects

14 Copyright © BNIM Architects

About Ecotone Publishing — The Green Building Publisher

Ecotone is an independent publishing company whose mission is to educate and provide examples of restorative design to people in the building industry. In nature, an ecotone is a biologically rich transition zone between two or more dissimilar ecosystems. For architecture, it is about understanding the richness of the boundaries between the habitats of people and the environment.

Ecotone — exploring the relationship between the built and natural environments.

For more information on Ecotone or to purchase other books please visit our website at:

www.ecotonedesign.com

or contact us at:

Ecotone LLC
P.O. Box 7147
Kansas City, Missouri
64113-0147

e-mail: info@ecotonedesign.com

Order Form

Ecotone Publishing

Books may be purchased by ordering on the Ecotone Website — www.ecotonedesign.com using any major credit card. Or by photocopying this order form and mailing it to us with a check made payable to Ecotone LLC. For bulk or academic orders please e-mail us at info@ecotone.com

Shipping Information
Please send all checks to Ecotone LLC

Ecotone LLC
P.O. Box 7147
Kansas City, Missouri
64113-0147

Shipping and Handling
All books are sent by regular mail. Please allow up to three weeks for delivery.

Title	Price	Quantity Amount
The Philosophy of Sustainable Design	$29.95 US / $40.95 CDN	———————
The Dumb Architect's Guide to Glazing Selection	$19.95 US / $24.95 CDN	———————
	Subtotal	———————
	Sales Tax (MO) add 6.92%	———————
	Shipping & Handling: $5.00 plus $0.50 each item	———————
	Total	———————

(Prices subject to change without notice)

Please fill out the following fields for **checks made payable to Ecotone LLC**
(for other methods of payment please visit the website listed above):

Ship To: _____

Address _____

City/State/Zip _____

Daytime Phone _____

e-mail address _____